IMAGES
of England

THE WEY & ARUN JUNCTION CANAL

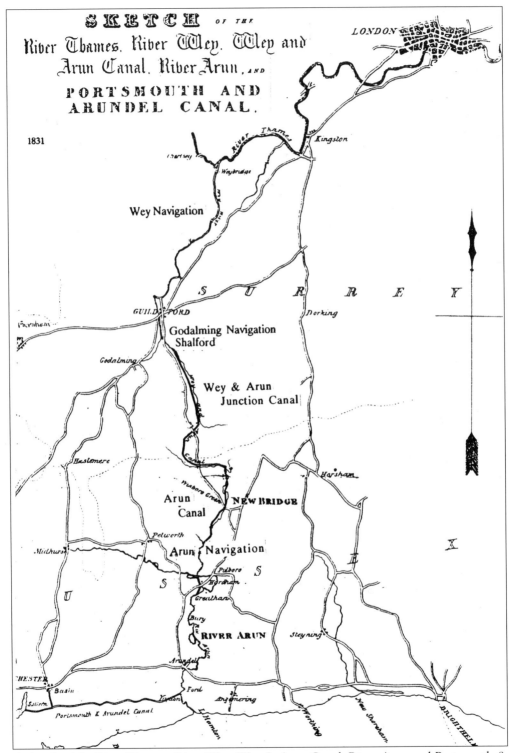

A sketch of the River Thames, River Wey, Wey & Arun Canal, River Arun and Portsmouth & Arundel Canal, 1831, showing the inland water route from the Thames to the English Channel.

2

IMAGES
of England

THE WEY & ARUN
JUNCTION CANAL

Compiled by
P.A.L. Vine

TEMPUS

First published 1999
Copyright © P.A.L. Vine, 1999

Tempus Publishing Limited
The Mill, Brimscombe Port,
Stroud, Gloucestershire, GL5 2QG

ISBN 0 7524 1721 5

Typesetting and origination by
Tempus Publishing Limited
Printed in Great Britain by
Midway Clark Printing, Wiltshire

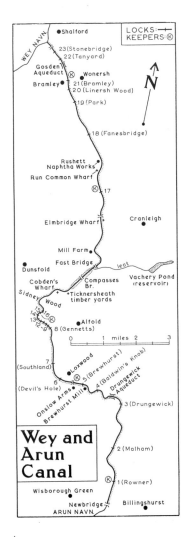

British Waterways – 2,000 miles of history

British Waterways runs the country's two-centuries-old working heritage of canals and river navigations. It conserves the historic buildings, structures and landscapes which blend to create the unique environment of the inland waterways, and protects their valuable and varied habitats.

As part of its commitment to the heritage of the waterways, British Waterways was instrumental in setting up The Waterways Trust, which aims to educate the public about the inland waterways and to promote the restoration and preservation of their rich architectural, historical and environmental heritage.

The Waterways Trust is a partnership between British Waterways, The National Waterways Museum at Gloucester, the Boat Museum at Ellesmere Port and the Canal Museum, Stoke Bruerne. The Trust cares for the National Waterways Collection, the country's pre-eminent collection of canal artefacts, documents and boats which are on view to the public at all the museums.

The Waterways Trust also manages the British Waterways Archive, a unique collection of inland waterway records dating back to the late seventeenth century and containing the largest documentary and photographic resource of its kind in Britain. Supported by the Heritage Lottery Fund, the archive is the subject of an ambitious project to make the collection available to all via the Internet. The new Cyber Archive will, for the first time, create a single catalogue of Britain's canal archives, revolutionizing research into the history of the inland waterways.

For more information about British Waterways call 01923 20 11 20 or visit the website at www.britishwaterways.co.uk.

For access to the archive, or to get up-to-date information about the Cyber Archive project, call 01452 318041.

Contents

ANNO QUINQUAGESIMO TERTIO

GEORGII III REGIS.

An ACT *for making and maintaining a Navigable Canal to unite the Rivers* Wey *and* Arun, *in the Counties of* Surrey *and* Sussex.

[1 APRIL 1813.]

WHEREAS the making and maintaining a Canal, navigable for Boats, Barges and other Veffels, from the River *Wey*, at or near to a certain place called *Stonebridge*, in the Parifh of *Shalford* in the County of *Surrey*, to the River *Arun*, at or near to a certain place called *Newbridge*, in the Parifh of *Wisborough Green* in the County of *Suffex*, in, to, or through the feveral Parifhes of *Shalford, Bramley, Wonerfh, Dunsfold, Cranley, Hascomb* and *Alfold*, or fome or one of them, in the County of *Surrey*; and alfo that part of the faid Parifh of *Alfold* which is fituate or lying in the faid County of *Suffex*, and in, to, or through the feveral Parifhes of *Kirdford, Wisborough Green, Rudgwick, Billingshurft,* and *Pulborough*, in the faid County of *Suffex*; would not only open a fhort, eafy

---

The preamble to the Wey & Arun Junction Canal Act, 1813. The Act empowered the company to raise capital, purchase land, collect tolls and place mileposts at half-mile intervals along the banks.

Introduction

For centuries the Surrey and Sussex rivers had formed an integral part of the counties' network of communications. Since the days of Queen Elizabeth, the Arun had been navigable for sea-going vessels up to Arundel; by an Act of 1651 locks were installed on the River Wey from the Thames to Guildford and continued to Godalming soon after the accession of King George III; before the Bastille had fallen the Arun Navigation had been extended by tunnel and canal to Wisborough Green. Thus, when the Wey & Arun Junction Canal was opened in 1816, the inland water route from London to the English Channel was complete.

The Act of Parliament, obtained in 1813, authorized the raising of £90,500 capital in £100 shares. The prospectus estimated local traffic at 30,000 tons, and hoped that one-twelfth, or 100,000 tons, of the London-Portsmouth trade would pass through the canal. The line involved the surmounting of few natural obstacles and digging began in July under the supervision of the engineer, Josias Jessop, one of the sons of William Jessop. Leaving the Wey by Stonebridge Wharf, Shalford, the waterway ascended through Bramley and Run Common to its summit level near Cranleigh by seven locks. Here it crossed the Surrey/Sussex watershed 165ft above sea-level, disappearing through a cutting at Alfold and crossing a valley into Sidney Wood. Then, descending rapidly through sixteen locks to Loxwood and the fertile pastures of Mallham and Rowner, it joined the Arun Canal at Newbridge.

The largest shareholder and chairman of the company was George O'Brien Wyndham, 3rd Earl of Egremont, who is better known for his patronage of art than for his £23,000 investment in this ambitious venture.

Work on the canal was seriously retarded by the discovery that the 2,000-yard cutting was through sand and by the bankruptcy of the contractor, Zachariah Keppell of Alfold. However, on 29 September 1816 the Wey & Arun Junction Canal was officially opened.

The third Earl of Egremont (1751-1837) painted by George Clint (1770-1854), c.1810. Lord Egremont was the Wey & Arun's largest shareholder and probably the richest man in the kingdom.

The Earl of Egremont, accompanied by the Mayor and Aldermen of Guildford, assembled before the Compasses Inn at Alfold, where, after providing a roasted ox and 200 gallons of ale for the 'navigators', they embarked on four gaily decorated barges. Then, accompanied by two bands and followed by a string of lighters loaded with coal and timber, they began the ten-mile voyage to Guildford. At Stonebridge the party was met by the barge of the Commissioners of the Godalming Navigation and together the procession entered the River Wey amid hearty cheering from the crowds lining the muddy banks. The *County Chronicle* described the colourful scene from St Catherine's Hill: 'The sunshine which now broke out, combined with the unrivalled scenery of the favourite spot, the music, and numerous assemblage of spectators, and the merry peal of the bells of Guildford; Shalford and Godalming, all heard at this time, gave an effect to the scene which could not be contemplated but with the most lively and pleasing emotions.'

After a civic welcome at Guildford, some 130 guests dined at a banquet given by the Company at the White Hart. 'And thus, said the *Times* correspondent, 'has opened under the happiest and most promising auspices, a canal, 18 miles in length, through a beautiful and picturesque country, to which it is as ornamental as it promises to be beneficial. A canal which not only promises great advantage to the proprietors, and to the counties of Surrey and Sussex from Arundel to London, but which with the addition of a very few miles at a trifling espense, will be highly beneficial to the public service, to the greatest naval arsenal in the kingdom, as well as to the private trade and opulence of Portsmouth and the city of Chichester.'

Petworth House, the seat of the Earl of Egremont, 1821. The boathouse on the lake can be seen in the left-hand corner. The park was landscaped by Lancelot 'Capability' Brown (1715-1783) in the 1750s.

But although the price of coal fell by 13s a chaldron in Guildford, trade was slow to develop. The cost of building the canal was £107,000 – £99,550 was raised by the issue of 905 shares of £100 at £110 each and the balance by mortgaging the tolls. Then, in 1821, the committee, in optimistic anticipation of the success of the Portsmouth & Arundel Canal, ordered a dividend of one per cent. However, the Portsmouth Canal proved a disastrous failure and in 1824, its most successful year, only 4,000 tons, not the hoped-for 100,000, were carried between Portsmouth, Chichester and London.

Trade was three times greater from London than from the coast; coal and groceries, and in smaller quantities porter and pottery, arrived regularly from the Thames, but consignments to the metropolis varied from timber, bark and hoops to more unusual items like furniture, soldiers' baggage, and Indian cotton. Exceptionally villagers would see barges guarded by redcoats carrying bullion bound for the Bank of England. One day in 1825, the *Union* and the *Portsea* went through together with seventy-two tons on board. Barges from Littlehampton and Arundel brought seaweed for the farms, beach for road repairs, grain for the watermills, and a wide variety of stores; they returned loaded with farm produce, flour, hoops and forest timber.

Through traffic was negligible when an impetus was given to trade towards the close of the 1830s by reducing the tolls. Receipts rose from £1,950 in 1835-1836 to £2,550 in 1839-40, but 23,000 tons was the most the canal was ever destined to

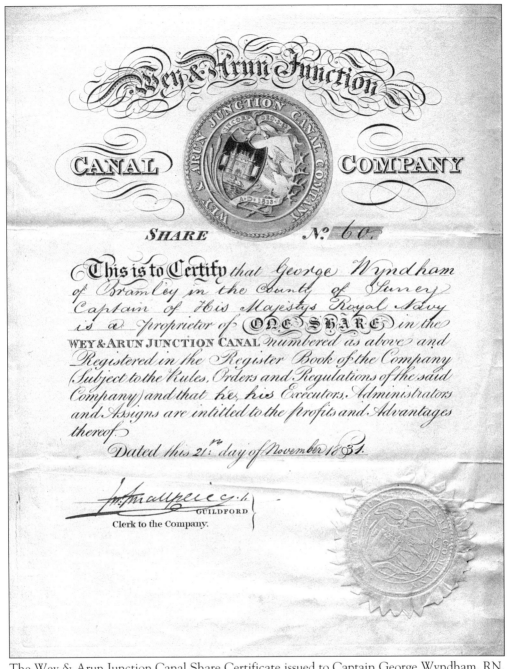

The Wey & Arun Junction Canal Share Certificate issued to Captain George Wyndham, RN, nephew of the 3rd Earl of Egremont. Each £100 share cost the original subscribers £110.

WEY AND ARUN JUNCTION CANAL.

Abstract of Account for the Year ending 1st May, 1834.

1833.	£	s	D	1834.	£	s	D
MAY 1. To Balance in the hands of the Treasurer ...	1055	10	4	APRIL 30. By Payments, viz.			
1834.				Clerk, Superintendant, Collectors, Lock-keepers, &c. Salaries	323	4	3
APRIL 30. Received for Tolls on the Canal during the Year	2157	18	4	Repairs and Incidental Charges	366	11	9
Rent for Wharfs, &c.	24	1	1	Rent, Taxes, Tithes, &c.	339	18	4
				William Burch for a new Windmill Pump	173	9	7
				George Rennie, Esq. for Survey and Report relative to increase of the Supply of Water	60	18	0
				Printing and Stationary	2	13	10
				Interest on Mortgage of Tolls	70	0	0
				Dividends paid on			
				8 Shares for 1828 .... 8 0 0			
				8 ———— 1829 .... 8 0 0			
				8 ———— 1830 .... 8 0 0			
				18 ———— 1831 .... 18 0 0			
				48 ———— 1832 .... 48 0 0			
				837 ———— 1833 ....837 0 0	927	0	0
					2263	15	9
				Balance in Treasurer's Hands	973	14	0
	3237	9	9		3237	9	9

Wey & Arun Canal Company Account, 1833-1834.

carry, for the railway era had begun. Canal receipts fell as all over the country tolls were reduced to competitive levels. Steam power was replacing that of sail, obviating the need for the safer, but more costly, inland passage by lessening the risk of shipwreck on the Goodwin Sands. The canal suffered besides from an acute water shortage on its summit level, which halted all cargoes during spells of dry weather, for neither the dredging of the fifty-acre reservoir, Vachery Pond nor the erection of two pump windmills satisfactorily solved the problem.

The payment of a dividend had been resumed in 1828, but it never rose higher than £1 per share, for the Company's mortgage was not finally paid off until 1842. The toll on coal fell by a shilling a ton on the opening of the London-Guildford railway in 1845, after which the dividends declined as receipts dropped – to 15s, 10s, 7s 6d, and in 1852 to 5s. Meanwhile the price of shares had tumbled as soon as it became evident that the navigation was not a profitable undertaking. By 1820 they had fallen to half their nominal value and a decade later to a third; in 1850 they fetched a bare ten pounds.

A sudden increase in tolls between 1856-1858 was occasioned by the canal's work in transporting rails and building materials for the construction of the Horsham-Petworth railway, opened in 1859. During 1863 and 1864 the canal ironically contributed to its own downfall by giving the same assistance to the Guildford-Horsham railway, opened in 1865. The railway followed the line of the waterway until near Cranleigh, crossing it by a viaduct at Whipley Manor. For this intrusion over canal property the Company received £600 compensation, which enabled them to pay a last dividend of 6s per share in 1865. Realising that they were unequal to the competition, the shareholders decided to go into liquidation.

RECEIVED the *3rd* day of *August* 1838. of the Treasurer of the WEY AND ARUN JUNCTION CANAL COMPANY, *Five* Pounds, being the Dividend of £1. per Cent. upon my Share of the said Canal, ordered at a Meeting of the Committee of Management of the said Canal, on the Twenty-second day of May last.

£5 - ~

A receipt for dividend payment, 1838.

The 3rd Earl's eighty-fourth birthday being celebrated in Petworth Park in 1835, from the painting by W.F. Witherington. Lord Egremont can be seen seated on horseback.

In 1868 there appeared a small book entitled *The Thames to the Solent by canal and sea, or the Log of the Una boat Caprice*. Its author, J.P. Dashwood, described the weedy and semi-derelict state of the canal in July 1867 and, remarking that the canal was about to be sold by auction, added, 'in fact, considering the great expense in procuring water and the small amount of traffic; it is impossible it can pay its way'. Attempts to close the canal were resisted, however, by both the Arun and the Godalming Navigations, who opposed the Abandonment Bill in the House of Lords and secured the insertion of seven additional clauses whose effect was to allow the waterway to be kept open if certain conditions were fulfilled. The shareholders therefore decided to put the canal up for auction as a going concern, but when the auction was held in London in August 1870 no bids were received for the canal. Since tolls continued to decline (in 1870-1871 they were under £300), an order was made to close the navigation in July 1871. Although in its fifty-five years of activity it failed to achieve trading renown, suffered many setbacks and enjoyed only a modicum of prosperity, the waterway remains unique in the annals of canal history as being the sole navigation to have linked London with the South Coast.

Between 1871 and 1910 it was the task of the official liquidator to sell back the bed of the canal to the riparian owners. This was a protracted affair as few

---

TOLLS CHARGED ON DIFFERENT GOODS,

ON THE WEY AND ARUN JUNCTION CANAL.

	S D	
Coal	at 2 0	per Ton for the whole line, [line.
	or 0 2⅓	per Ton per Mile, not to exceed 2s 3d for the whole
Timber, Hoops, Bark, and Corn..	at 2 3	per Ton for the whole line,
	or 0 2½	per Ton per Mile, not to exceed 2s 3d per Ton for the whole line.
Grocery	at 2 3	per Ton for the whole line,
	or 0 2½	per Ton per Mile.
Fire Wood	at 1 1½	per Ton for the whole line,
	or 0 1½	per Ton per Mile, not to exceed 1s 1½d per Ton for the whole line.
Chalk and Lime	at 0 1¼	per Ton per Mile.
Manure from London	at 0 1	per Ton per Mile for the whole line.
Sea Gravel and Sea Weed	at 1 0	per Ton for the whole line,
	or 0 1	per Ton per Mile, not to exceed 1s per Ton for the whole line.

Light Barges 1s at each of the first Locks at each end of the line of Canal.

	S D	DURING SHORT WATER.
Timber, Hoops, Bark, & Corn,		
In Barges not having 15 Tons	at 4 6	per Ton for the whole line,
	or 0 3	per Ton per Mile, not to exceed 4s 6d per Ton for the whole line
Except as back carriage to pass	at 2 3	per Ton for the whole line,
	or 0 2⅓	per Ton per Mile, not to exceed 2s 3d per Ton for the whole line.

Light Barges 1s at each of the Three Locks at each end of the Line of Canal.

Guildford 1st June 1844   *John Smallpeice clerk*   [Russells, Printers.]

When the canal was opened the toll on coal was 4d a ton mile or 6s for passing the whole line. In the hope of attracting more traffic, this was reduced to 3s in May 1822. The opening of the railway to Guildford in 1844 prompted a further reduction to 2s and finally to 1s a ton in June 1855. This last reduction caused an upsurge in traffic with tolls increasing by a third and tonnage by half.

A Guildford coal merchants' advertisement, c.1850.

Although a towpath existed along the length of the Wey & Arun Junction Canal, pleasure boaters found that on part of the Arun navigation no towpath existed and obnoxious field gates created problems for horse towage.

One of the problems confronting commercial traffic was unexpected delays caused by water shortages. By 1822 this was so apparent that increased tolls were charged on cargoes of less than thirty tons. When traffic was heaviest in the 1830s, carts were used to lighten barge loads between locks when there was insufficient draught. The advent of pleasure boating in the 1860s heightened this problem with the result that in 1866 no pleasure boat or steamer could pass without a pilot. In this 1868 illustration the boat is aground in the Godalming Navigation at Unstead because the local mill was undergoing repairs and the boating party had to wait until the miller was prepared to allow water to come down.

landowners wanted to take possession of what they regarded as a stagnant ditch even when it was offered to them at a nominal price. As a result some stretches of the old waterway were simply abandoned to form a melancholy and picturesque part of the landscape. Soon its weed-covered bed became a haunt of waterfowl and wildlife and a favourite walk for the countryside explorer.

Many decades passed before the first serious effort to reopen the canal came in 1970 with the formation of the Wey & Arun Canal Society, later to become the Wey & Arun Canal Trust. This body now has over 1,200 voting members and has been very successful in fundraising and in obtaining sponsorship from both local organizations and the public. The trust has been responsible for clearing and dredging almost half the eighteen miles of canal bed, putting seven locks back into working order and rebuilding numerous bridges and culverts.

The Shalford Natural History Society cleared and repaired Tanyard Bridge at Gosden in 1977. Similarly the Pulborough Society was among those who contributed to the cost of rebuilding Pallingham Quay Bridge which was reopened in 1976. Before the whole line of the former waterway can be restored, however, certain difficulties remain to be overcome, since some landowners who now own

OF THE

WEY & ARUN JUNCTION
CANAL PROPERTY,

AS A GOING CONCERN,

COMPRISING THE

LINE OF CANAL EXTENDING FROM STONE-BRIDGE,

ONLY A SHORT DISTANCE FROM THE IMPORTANT

Market Town of Guildford to New Bridge at Pulborough,

Forming the connecting link between the Navigable Rivers the Wey and the Arun, thereby affording direct Water Communication between the Port of Littlehampton, and the Town of Arundel, in the County of Sussex, and the River Thames, passing through sundry Parishes in the Counties of Surrey and Sussex, a distance of about 18 miles, which, with the Banks, Reservoirs, Wharves, Buildings, and the Appurtenances attached, occupy an Area of

ABOUT 200 ACRES,

ALSO

IN THE TOWN OF GUILDFORD,

VALUABLE FREEHOLD PREMISES,

CONSISTING OF

A RESIDENCE AND BUILDINGS,

With Timber and Slate Merchants' and Stone Masons' Yards;

Which will be Offered by Auction, by

HENRY CRAWTER,

(The Person appointed by the Vice-Chancellor, Sir Richard Malins)

AT THE MART, TOKENHOUSE YARD, LONDON,

On TUESDAY, the 30th AUGUST, 1870,

At TWELVE o'clock precisely, in FOUR LOTS.

Particulars may be had of Messrs. W. H., M. & F. F. SMALLPEICE, Solicitors, Guildford; of Messrs. PYKE, IRVING, & PYKE, Solicitors, No. 43, Lincoln's Inn Fields, W.C.; at the "White Hart" Inn, Guildford; Principal Inns at Cranley, Pulborough, and other Inns in the Neighbourhood of the Canal; at the Mart; and of the AUCTIONEER, No. 5, Bedford Row, W.C.

N.B.—Particulars can also be had of Mr. WILLIAM STANTON, at the Wharf, Bramley, Manager of the Canal, and Wharfinger, and who will shew the Property.

When the canal was put up for auction in 1870 no bid was received for the waterway.

The final order to close the canal was made in July 1871.

Wey and Arun Junction Canal.

In Chancery.

In the matter of the Companies Act, 1862,
and
In the matter of the Company of the Proprietors of the Wey and Arun Junction Canal.

BY AN ORDER made by his Honor the Vice Chancellor, SIR RICHARD MALINS, in Chambers in the above matter, dated the 26th day of May, 1871, on the application of the Official Liquidator of the above named Company, it was ordered as follows : "It is ordered that Notice be inserted in the *London Gazette*, the *Times Newspaper*, the *West Sussex Gazette*, the *Surrey Standard* Newspaper, and the *Surrey Advertiser* Newspaper; and by Bills posted in the Towns of *Arundel* and *Guildford*, and along the Route of the said Canal, that an application has been made to the Court for the closing for traffic of the said Canal (extending from Stonebridge in the Parish of Shalford, in the County of Surrey, to Newbridge in the Parish of Wisborough Green, in the County of Sussex, the property of the above named Company), and the extinguishment of all rights of way, or user, and other rights in reference thereto, or in connection therewith, on or after the 1st day of July next: And that such application will be further heard and considered on the 24th day of June next, at the Chambers of the said Judge, No. 3, Stone Buildings, Lincolns Inn, in the County of Middlesex, at 12 of the Clock at noon: And it is ordered that the said application be adjourned for further consideration to the said 24th day of June next, at the place and time aforesaid, with a view to the Court then making an Order in accordance with the application or such other Order as the Judge may think to be proper under the circumstances."

J. A. BUCKLEY,
Chief Clerk.

W. STENT, PRINTER, 32, HIGH STREET, GUILDFORD.

part of the canal bed do not wish a public right of way to divide their land. The fact that a large housing estate has been built upon the canal bed at Bramley will also necessitate a new line of waterway being cut. The prospects for the navigation being fully restored were assessed by Sir William Halcrow & Partners in 1992 who confirmed that there were no insurmountable obstacles preventing complete restoration. This remains the trust's aim.

The first excursion boat was launched in 1994 and after the rebuilding of Brewhurst and Baldwins Knob locks was completed, regular canal cruises began to operate between Loxwood and Drungewick in 1998.

The immediate task is to raise funds for the new aqueduct and road bridge at Drungewick, which is likely to cost £600,000. When this work has been completed it should not be too long before the canal is reopened through the already restored locks at Drungewick, Mallam and Rowner to its terminal point at Newbridge, a distance of six miles.

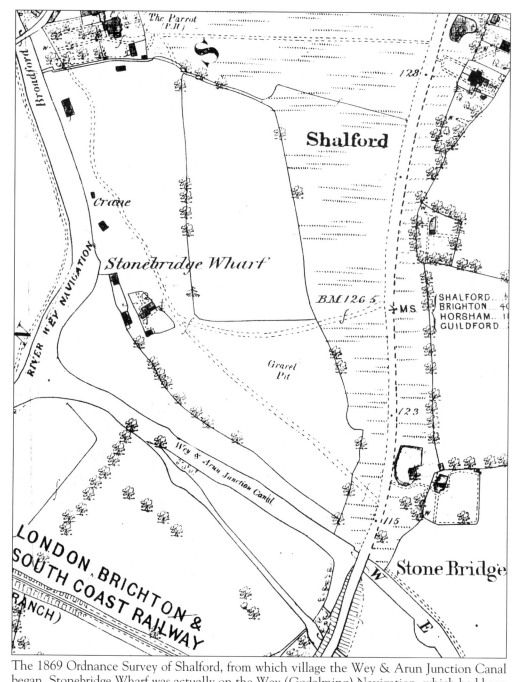

The 1869 Ordnance Survey of Shalford, from which village the Wey & Arun Junction Canal began. Stonebridge Wharf was actually on the Wey (Godalming) Navigation, which had been opened in 1763.

One
Shalford to Bramley

Gunpowder being loaded c.1900 at Stonebridge Wharf, Shalford. The red warning flag is flying from the barge. The powder was brought by horse-drawn waggon from Chilworth Mills and stored in the wooden warehouse standing on staddle stones at right. In the 1830s cargoes totalled about 100 tons a year, which increased to 300 tons during the Crimean War and in 1873 exceeded 500 tons. In August 1864 a newly delivered barge belonging to Samuel Sharpe of Chilworth – the last to be built at the Pallingham boatyard – had been loaded with gunpowder at Stonebridge Wharf, and was only a mile or so from the wharf when it exploded. The two men on board were blown to pieces and the vessel sank. These dangerous cargoes continued to be carried by water to the magazines at Woolwich, Purfleet, and Barking Creek until 1921. The low headroom of Broadlford Bridge (centre left) was a notorious bottleneck when the river was high.

A closer view of Stonebridge Wharf taken *c*.1865 shows a laden timber barge with collapsible mast. The masts were required for barges navigating the lower reaches of the Thames, where there was no continuous horse towing path.

The derelict wharf at Stonebridge in 1952. After the Chilworth powder traffic ceased only two barges regularly worked the river above Guildford between the First and Second World Wars. The coal traffic ceased in 1946 and no cargo has been unloaded at the wharf since 1950.

Situated north of the wharf, the Parrot Inn in Shalford was a favourite stopping place for bargemen working between the Wey Navigation and the Wey & Arun Junction Canal. The building has not changed a great deal since this view was taken in 1952 but it is now popular with pleasure boaters.

Above, below and opposite (top): It is interesting to compare these three views of the entrance to the Bramley stream where it joins the Godalming Navigation at Shalford. The first was taken in 1946, the second in 1952 when moorings first began to be available, and the third in 1984, by which time the spot had become, as it is today, extremely popular for use by cruisers and houseboats. This junction was known as the Gun's Mouth, an allusion to the time when barges were moored here before being loaded with gunpowder at Stonebridge Wharf.

Until the 1950s the approach to the first bridge over the junction canal remained much as it had always been. Canoes and punts could still be dragged through the silted entrance to the private gardens bordering the canal beyond.

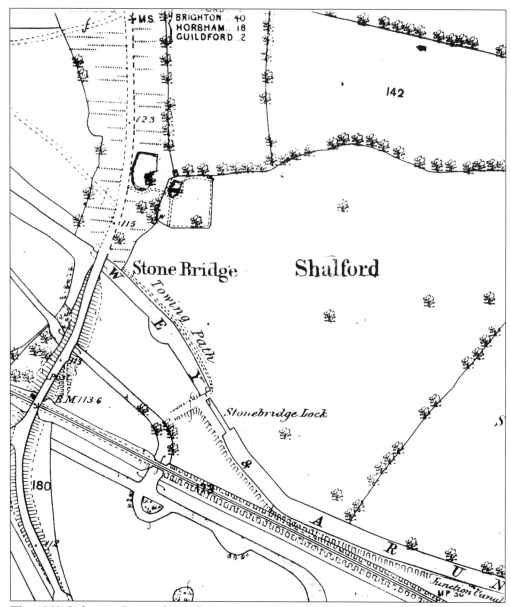

The 1869 Ordnance Survey shows the entrance to the canal at Stonebridge and the approach to the first lock. The lock has ceased to be marked on the 1895 survey and by 1934 houses had been built along the north side of the canal as far as the lock.

Increasing traffic along the former turnpike road from Guildford (now the A281) necessitated major renovation work to Stonebridge leaving only a culvert to replace the archway.

The approach to the site of Stonebridge Lock in 1952. The footbridges link the gardens of the private residences which are divided by the old canal.

The Stonebridge Lock site in 1952. All traces of the chamber have now vanished and only a change in levels denotes its former location. Now that the access to the cut has been closed, boats have to be moored in the Bramley stream.

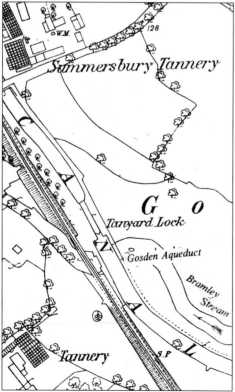

The 1869 Ordnance Survey showing the location of Tanyard Lock and the aqueduct over the Bramley stream at Gosden. The tanneries at Gosden received cargoes of bark, hides and skins by water and dispatched much of their produce likewise. Today the canal bed has been levelled and no trace of the tanneries remains.

The Guildford to Horsham railway at Gosden is seen running parallel to the former canal bed in 1964. The canal bridge is centre right with the site of Summersbury Tanyard behind. The railway, opened in 1865, had driven away the canal's remaining traffic by 1871 and was itself closed in its centenary year of 1965.

The bridge over the canal at Gosden Common, Shalford, in 1964. When the Guildford to Horsham railway was built the road bridge over the railway was extended over the canal (far parapet) and incorporated the canal bridge, built in 1815, which enabled horses to cross from one side of the towpath to the other.

The Shalford Conservation Society restored the brickwork of Gosden Canal Bridge and cleared the heavily overgrown site. Here the author is seen taking part in the reopening ceremony held in October 1977. (Photograph courtesy of the *Surrey Advertiser*).

Gosden Aqueduct, which carried the canal over the Bramley Stream, was immediately to the south of Tanyard Lock. The brick aqueduct was the first to be built in Surrey. Its bed and the channel between Summersbury Tannery and the lock were filled in before 1895. This view was taken in 1952.

A closer view of the four-arched aqueduct seen from the Bramley Stream in 1999.

Gosden Aqueduct seen from below the iron girder bridge of the former Guildford to Horsham railway in 1964. After the railway was closed in 1965 the bridge was dismantled. It is strange that the brickwork of the aqueduct is in much poorer condition there than on the opposite side.

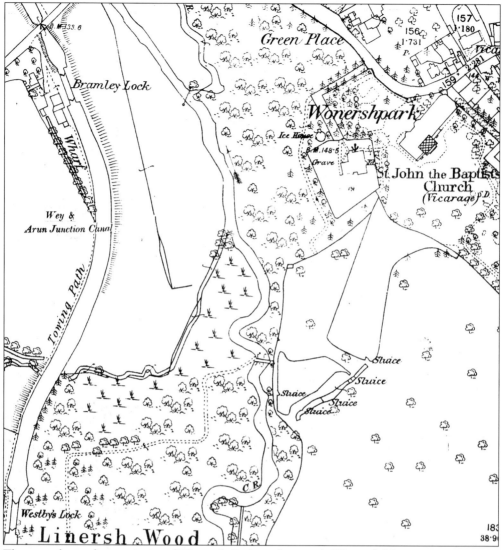

The map shows the proximity of Wonersh Park to the canal. Wonersh House was a mansion described by Brayley as being a 'spacious structure of red brick with an arcade and convenient offices.' The dining room was 42ft by 25ft and 22ft high and the library 62ft in length. Bramley Wharf was exactly a quarter of a mile from the western end of the house but Westby's Lock was 700 yards away looking over the lake towards Linersh Wood. Since this 1871 survey all the remains of the two locks have vanished and Linersh Wood is now a respectable housing estate.

Two

Bramley to Cranleigh

Wharf Cottage at Bramley, c.1868. William Stanton, wharfinger, lockkeeper and coal merchant, is in the top hat. When he died in 1872 aged sixty-one he bequeathed a legacy of £1,000 to the villagers of Bramley, the interest of which provided for the distribution of coal to the poor at Christmas. His obituary referred to his many admirable traits of character and acts of benevolence, one of which was to allow pleasure boater J.B. Dashwood the 'run of his kitchen garden, rich in gooseberries and currants.' The coal pens lie shaded beneath a line of trees. The edge of the lock is visible in the right foreground. *Active* was the last barge to pass through Bramley Lock on 27 June 1872.

Bramley Wharf Cottage had been enlarged by 1952 but the bricks and coping stone from the lock had been removed before the turn of the twentieth century. A Mr R. Halliday wrote in his copy of Dashwood's book that he had been to Bramley in June 1914 to inspect the site of the canal and sadly recorded that there 'was no trace of the lock'. In the 1940s, when the cottage was occupied by Mrs Mott, her grandson, Mr Batten, dug up an iron milestone in the garden bearing the inscription 'Arun 5 1/2' (*Surrey Times*, June 1949). This would originally have been sited 5 1/2 miles from Newbridge near Brewhurst Lock, Loxwood.

It was to the Grantley Arms in Wonersh that the Dashwood family repaired after their frustrating journey by boat from Guildford to Bramley. However, their derogatory opinion of the inn in 1867 is in no way reciprocated today.

The entrance lodge to Bramley House (now demolished), which was the home of shareholder Captain Wyndham, RN, (1786-1845), the 4th Earl of Egremont and nephew of the third earl, who inherited the earldom but not his wealth. After the earl's death in 1845 it became the home of Mr Edward Jekyll, father of the garden designer Gertrude Jekyll (1843-1932), who lived there from the age of five until 1868.

One of the first instances of the canal being used for pleasure boat excursions is the invitation from Lord and Lady Grantley of Wonersh House to the two Miss Talbots to travel by boat from Guildford to Wonersh for a *fete champetre* in May 1831.

LORD & LADY GRANTLEY *with* **Mr. C. F. NORTON** *request the Pleasure of the two Miss Talbots' Company to a Fête Champêtre, at Wonersh, on Thursday, the 26th Instant, at Two o'Clock.*

Wonersh, 18th May, 1831.

....

*** *It is requested that this Card may be delivered at the Porter's Lodge.*

Boats will be provided to convey the Company to Wonersh, and will start from Guildford Bridge at One o'Clock precisely.

N. B.---In the event of the Day fixed for the Fête proving unfavorable, it will be postponed to the following Day.

Wonersh House was the country seat of the Norton family when this drawing was made, *c*.1840.
William Norton, the 2nd Lord Grantley (1740-1822) was colonel of the 1st Royal Surrey
Regiment of Militia and strongly opposed the building of the canal on the grounds that it would
ruin his deer park. His opposition to the bill was only overcome by the company agreeing to pay
compensation of £2,000 which it noted in its accounts was for building a wall stipulated to be built
in his Lordship's park, but which his Lordship never intended to erect. Ironically, his nephew the

third baron was, in 1860, to oppose the building of the Guildford to Horsham railway on the grounds that it would do inestimable harm to his property. To the argument that the waterway passed closer to his house than the proposed railway he contended that the canal had an ornamental appearance rather than the reverse and affirmed that it was made to curve through his park for the purpose of affording a rather more pleasing view than a straight stretch of water. The house was sold to the Sudbury family in 1885 and was demolished in 1929.

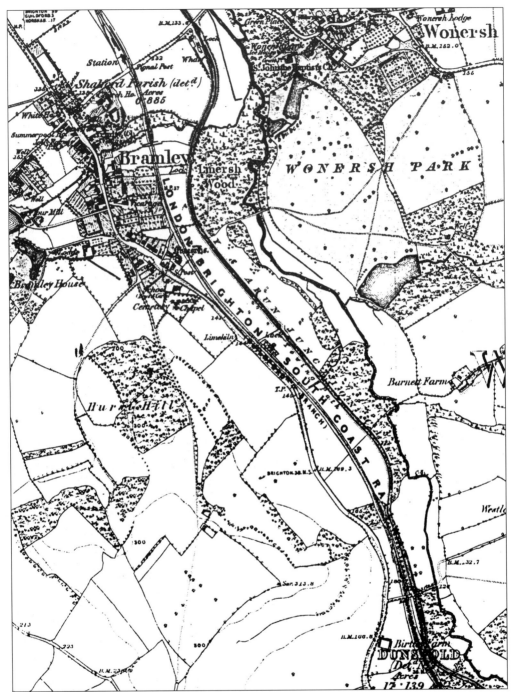

This six inch Ordnance Survey of 1871 shows how closely the newly opened Guildford to Horsham railway hugged the line of the canal between Bramley and Birtley. Although the canal company hoped in 1859 to persuade the London, Brighton & South Coast Railway to convert the canal into a railway to link Guildford with Pulborough, the railway company replied that they were only interested if the proposal had the support of the landowners who would undertake to sell the land at agricultural prices.

The canal bed in 1952 where it formerly passed through Lord Grantley's estate. It now forms part of the front gardens of houses on the Linersh Wood Estate.

A latter day view in 1999 of the site of the canal bed on the Linersh Wood Estate. The prospect of restoring this section of the canal is unlikely but it may be possible to make a new channel by using the Bramley Stream as far as Birtley.

Water lilies cover the channel at Birtley in 1934. The great charm of abandoned canals is the way nature adorns their commercial features with flora of every description. Dashwood commented on the scenery here in 1867: 'The canal winds its way under the shade of woods on each side, which come quite down to the water's edge, where the water-lilies, both white and yellow, were floating in profusion.'

A primitive footbridge across the Birtley pound in 1946. Its origin remains unknown.

The canal was often frozen solid. The *West Sussex Gazette* reported in January 1871 that in spite of the thaw the canal was so frozen as to render navigation impossible. At Birtley the ice was nearly five inches thick. When a barge captain and his mate attempted to break the ice with heavy hammers 'they could not make the slightest impression'. This view was taken in 1954 after dredging and restocking had been carried out by the Bramley, Wonersh & Shamley Green Angling Association.

The Birtley Embankment, which rose some 40ft higher than the adjacent meadowland, seen here in 1979. It had twice to be repaired after the bank had been breached by heavy rain, first in 1976 and then again a couple of years later.

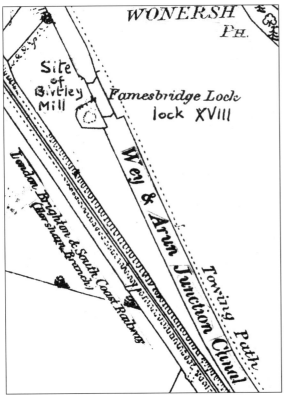

Birtley Mill had been built adjoining Lock XVIII at Fanesbridge in 1833 by William Burch to replace water lost through lockage. A second pump windmill stood by Lock XVII at Rowly Farm. In 1853 the materials of both mills were auctioned and sold so that by 1870 when the canal itself was put up for sale, the only reminder of their existence was the mention in the auction particulars of the site of the windmill by Lock XVIII which measured 8 perches.

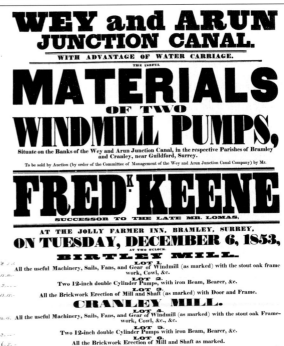

A poster advertising the sale of Birtley and Cranley Windmills, 1853. The auction was held at the Jolly Farmer Inn in Bramley. The materials of the two mills, which had cost over £1,000 to build, fetched £54.

The grass-grown, dried-up channel at Rushett Common in 1952 where the canal ran parallel to the Guildford to Horsham railway. The two-carriage train is drawn by a former LB & SCR tank engine built in the 1880s. On the site of the parish boundary, *i.e.* where some buildings stand above the engine's chimney, stood James Tickner's vinegar works in the mid-nineteenth century.

This view taken from beneath the Guildford to Horsham railway bridge shows the site of the vinegar works at Rushett which was one of the few local industries established adjacent to the canal.

The farm building marks the former site of James Tickner's vinegar works. The bridge in the background at right carried the former Guildford to Horsham railway over the lane leading to the canal.

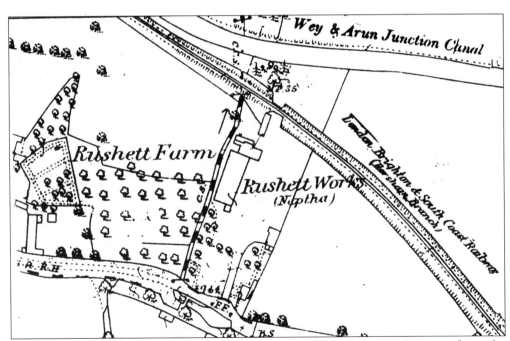

The prominent marking of the naptha factory on the 1871 Ordnance Survey reflects the importance of the business and shows its proximity to the canal and the Guildford to Horsham railway which had been opened in 1865. Rushett Common is a hamlet two miles south of Bramley.

The dry bed of the canal as it is today at Rushett Farm. Although barges carrying raw materials for the vinegar works discharged some of their cargoes here, there was no wharf and so most were unloaded at Run Common.

Close at hand to Rushett Farm was the charcoal furnace belonging to Richard Medland which burnt some 2,000 tons of cordwood annually to obtain charcoal for use in the production of naptha and acetic acid. As local timber became scarce, wood had to be brought from further afield. When loaded at Slinfold, for instance, it had either to be carted to Newbridge or to Loxwood and taken to the wharf at Run Common, seen here in 1952.

Run Common Wharf and winding hole has hardly changed in appearance since 1952, as this 1999 picture shows.

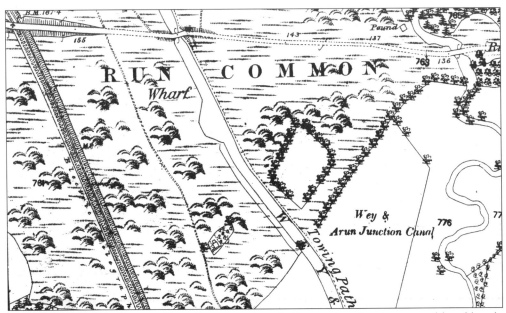

The 1870 Ordnance Survey of Run Common gives the impression that it was a wild and lonely place. William Cobbett passed over the canal bridge while riding from Hascombe to Ewhurst in August 1823 through what he termed the Weald of Surrey, where he considered only three things grew well – grass, wheat and oak trees.

'From time to time, we had to open small iron drawbridges', wrote Dashwood in 1867. Remains of this iron swing bridge straddled the bed at Whipley Manor in 1952, but the Surrey Industrial History Group determined in April 1981 from its circular ball-race, which measured three feet across, that it could not originally have been in this position. It was in fact moved a furlong or so southwards at the time the Guildford to Horsham railway was being built in the early 1860s.

When the London, Brighton & South Coast Railway built a viaduct over the canal at Whipley Manor in 1864, the company had to pay £600 compensation to the canal company for having to realign the towpath. The viaduct was removed after the railway was closed in 1965. This view was taken in 1952.

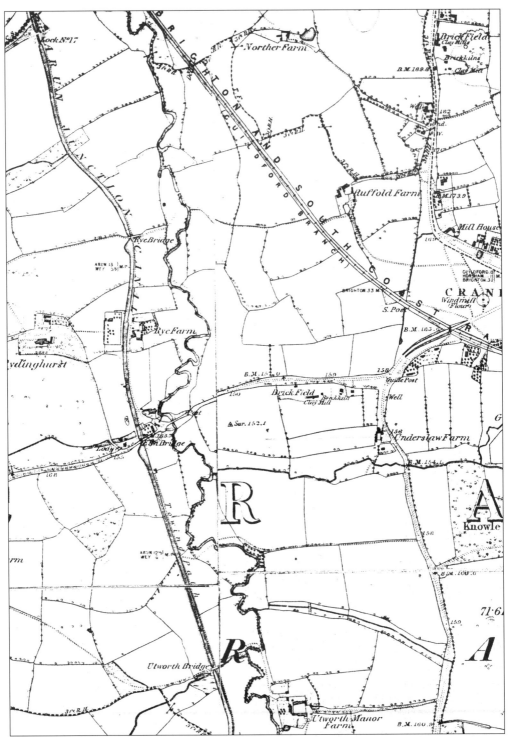

The summit level begins at Lock XVII and stretches for over five miles at a height of $162\frac{3}{4}$ ft above sea level. The length between Elm and Utworth bridges was one of the straightest on the waterway. (See p.51)

Lock XVII, located near Rowly Farm, Cranleigh, is marked on the Ordnance Survey of 1871. What is not marked is the site of Cranley (*sic*) windmill, erected by the lock in 1833 to improve the canal's water supply by pumping water drawn down back into the five-mile summit level. The mill, constructed of oak and cast iron, stood on a brick foundation and rose to a height of 16ft. It was dismantled in 1854.

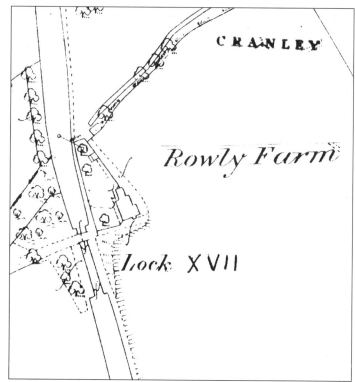

Lock XVII in 1963 before restoration. It is curious how disused canals were for many years the dumping ground of old bicycles, wash basins, water tanks and all manner of paraphernalia.

47

Left and below: Restoration of Lock XVII was well advanced when photographed in 1982. The Wey & Arun Trust's voluntary working parties laboured long and hard clearing debris from the lock chamber and rebuilding the walls. By 1986 the lock had been rebuilt.

Three
Cranleigh to Alfold

Elm Bridge at Cranleigh. The superintendent's cottage stood on the north side of the bridge. Thomas Pullen lived here in the 1860s and was alleged, in the course of evidence heard by the House of Lords Committee considering the bill for the canal's abandonment in 1868, to have 'kept a shop or something of that kind'. His services were, according to the clerk of the Arun Navigation, 'entirely useless'. The wharf assumed a greater importance to Cranleigh than might have been anticipated. This was due to the prohibitive tolls charged for road carriage as a consequence of goods having to pass through four turnpike gates between Guildford and Horsham. Coal which came up to the wharf was sold for about 30s a ton.

WEY & ARUN NAVIGATION. £5 REWARD

WHEREAS, on Sunday the 13th day of August instant, a quantity of the COPING on ELM BRIDGE was maliciously removed and injured;

NOTICE IS HEREBY GIVEN, that any Person who will give Information to Mr. STANTON, the Superintendent of the Navigation, so as to lead to the Conviction of the Offender or Offenders, shall receive a Reward of £5.

W. HAYDON SMALLPEICE,
CLERK.

Guildford,
15th August, 1848.

(Russells, Printers and Stationers.)

Damage to canal company property was not uncommon. If the bargee was the known culprit, restitution was sought from the bargemaster, but in other cases rewards had to be offered as was the case at Elm Bridge in 1848.

Views of the summit level in the spring, summer and winter of 1952 showing the straight between Utworth and Elm Bridges, Cranleigh. During periods of fine weather or above-average commercial activity the draught along the summit level was so reduced that either traffic was totally stopped or barges had to be partially off-loaded and cargoes transferred to horse and cart.

Mill Farm at Hascombe, viewed here in 1952, stands on the banks of the canal. To its right is the former mill-stream emanating from Vachery Pond. There is no evidence to show when the mill ceased to function but it is probable that it was before the canal was opened in 1816, since it does not appear in the schedule of buildings affected by the line of the proposed canal, nor has any reference been found to the canal company paying compensation. Certainly there is no trace of the mill race and sluices which suggests that the mill ceased to operate before the canal was built.

This 1952 photograph shows the overspill weir from the canal's summit level south of Mill Farm passing beneath the towpath and flowing into the Bramley Stream. In times of abnormally heavy rainfall a constant watch would be maintained to ensure that the paddles were sufficiently raised to prevent the canal banks bursting or overflowing.

Viewed from the north in 1953, this bridge by Fastbridge Farm was the last remaining original bridge over the summit level. It was built in 1815. The towpath passed beneath the bridge on the right bank.

Fast Bridge at Alfold was restored by the Wey & Arun Canal Trust in 1993. Much of the original brickwork was retained and a dam was constructed on the southern side to control the water level.

Compasses Bridge at Alfold Crossways. It was from this point on 29 September 1816, the day appointed for the official opening, that the Earl of Egremont and the mayor and aldermen of Guildford embarked on four gaily decorated barges. Lined up behind were eight boats laden with coal and timber while two bands entertained the procession as it wended its way to Guildford.

The Three Compasses at Alfold Crossways. While the Earl of Egremont and the company's guests were dining at the White Hart in Guildford, the navigators who had dug the canal devoured a roasted ox and drank two hundred gallons of ale outside the Compasses Inn on the night of the official opening.

This 1871 map shows the position of the five bridges which crossed the canal from Fast Bridge to Tickners Heath.

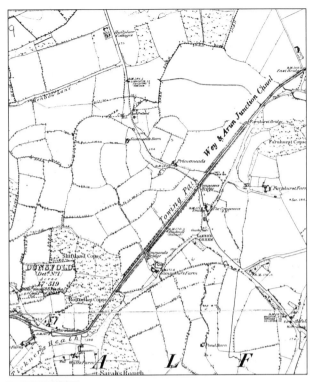

The summit level at Alfold looking south from Compasses Bridge in 1934. After over sixty years disuse, exploring the old canal had become a pastime for nature lovers. On 4 September 1936 *The Times* published a nostalgic article on the canal and included on the back page a half-page photograph showing the lily covered channel as pictured here.

Opposite: Vachery Pond provided the main water supply to the summit level. The original pond, once used as a hammer pond in connection with the extensive ironworks centred at Cranleigh, was enlarged by throwing a great wall of clay across the western end and building an embankment round the remainder to form a substantial lake covering over fifty acres. The overflow fed the stream which flowed through Hammer, Waterbridge, Bridge and Bookerslee Farms, where a sluice and tumbling bay controlled the water levels. A feeder channel wound round the fields and after passing under the Horsham to Guildford turnpike led into the canal through a culvert 150yds south of Fast Bridge. In spite of numerous efforts to improve the water supply by dredging the reservoir and raising the banks still further, the supply remained inadequate during dry periods. When George Rennie visited the area in July 1833 he noted that Vachery pond was too shallow and that, as it was sited nearly two miles from the canal, the small difference in levels caused the flow to be inadequate to maintain the five mile summit pound. Even when the reservoir was full the difference in water levels was little more than twenty feet. As it was the only regular source of supply (the remainder coming from springs and field drains), when the reservoir level fell, barges had to be lightened by transferring goods to lighters or to land carriage between Cranleigh and Alfold.

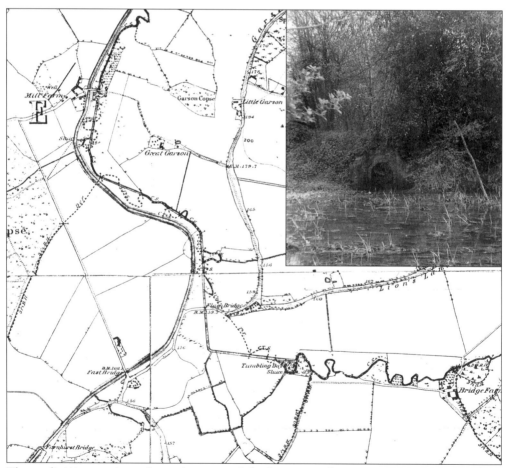

These adjoining sections of map show part of the long, meandering water course running from Vachery Pond to the canal. The inset picture is of the summit level at Alfold in 1964. This is

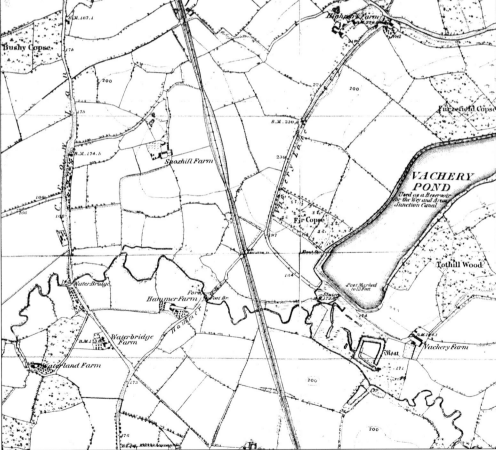

the point, south of Fastbridge, where the $2\frac{1}{2}$-mile feeder conduit from the fifty-acre Vachery Pond Reservoir flowed into the canal.

Summit level, Alfold. It was here that the deepest cutting had to be made and once the initial excavation had been completed 2,000yds of the bed was found to be of sand. This had to be doubly puddled with clay at great extra expense. This winter view taken in 1953 shows the depth of the cutting but the towpath on the right has disappeared.

Farnhurst Bridge was one of the original brick bridges along the summit level still standing in 1963. Note the towpath at right.

Alfold Mill, *c.*1905. The smock mill stood above the cutting on the east bank of the canal between Compasses and Simmond's bridges. It operated between 1820 and 1870 and was demolished in 1913. It has yet to be established whether there was a tunnel leading from the canal into the base of the mill or whether barges were loaded by crane or chute, since the water level was some distance below the ground level of the mill.

After the canal was closed in 1871, the official liquidator attempted to sell back the bed of the canal to the riparian owners. By 1901 he had succeeded in disposing of all but eight of the 200 acres but when the company was finally dissolved in 1910 there was still no indication of whether seven remaining parcels of land had found purchasers. The above stretch near Roundles Copse appeared to have no owner in 1952 although occupied by frogs, water lilies and all manner of waterfowl.

The Wey & Arun Canal Trust has cleared the winding hole at Cobden's Farm, Alfold, where barges formerly moored two and three abreast at this important centre of the brick trade.

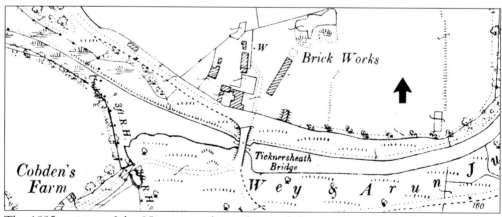

The 1895 revision of the 25in survey shows the weeds beginning to encroach upon the west side of Ticknersheath Bridge. Cobden's Farm had its own private wharf at which timber and agricultural produce were regularly loaded. Opposite was the brickworks established when the canal was being built in 1814.

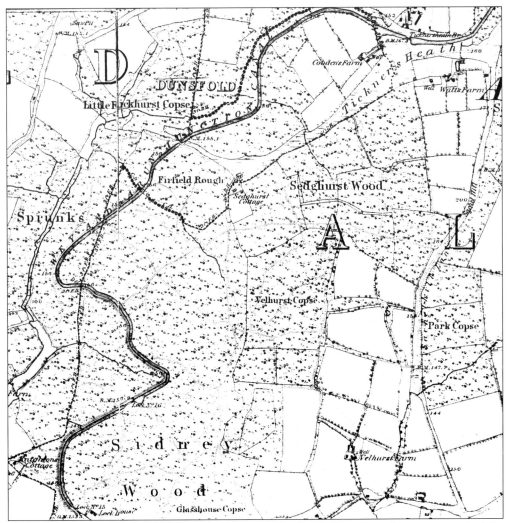

The twisting nature of the Wey & Arun Junction Canal is well evidenced from a perusal of the 1871 Ordnance Survey. Lock XV marks the end of the summit pound. Glasshouse Copse is a reminder that in the sixteenth century the Sidney Wood Glass House was an important centre of the Surrey glass industry. It produced the finest vessel glass known to the English forest glass industry.

The channel through Sidney Wood had not been touched for over one hundred years until the present owners, the Forestry Commission, gave permission for the canal bed to be cleared of the patchwork of trees and undergrowth. As the site is now designated to be of special scientific interest, the cut timber has to remain in place to encourage flora and insect life. However the tree stumps are in the process of being removed.

The twisting channel through Sidney Wood necessitated crossing numerous valleys whose streams had to be culverted thirty or forty feet beneath the canal bed. This broken culvert is a typical example of those still in place awaiting restoration.

Right and below: These two drawings by artist Donald Maxwell in 1923 are the only known illustrations of the locks in Sidney Wood before they were demolished for their materials in the latter part of the 1920s. No trace of the locks remains except for a difference in levels.

In the depths of Sidney Wood there are still sections of the canal which have remained undisturbed by barges for nearly 130 years. Impenetrable to the countryside explorer in late summer, these thickets give way to canopies of primroses and bluebells in the spring. Dashwood wrote in 1867: 'Our route now lay through a most refreshing and picturesque country of a broken and undulating character, densely clothed with a forest of oak trees, opening out and giving peeps into deep hollows verdant with luxuriant ferns and purple heather.'

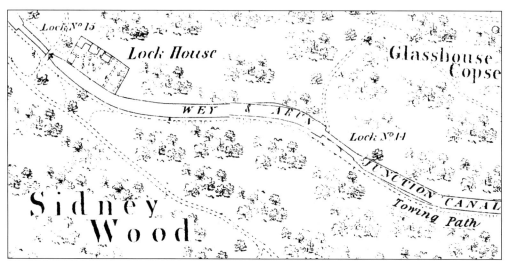

The lock house in Sidney Wood as depicted on the 1871 Ordnance Survey. The buildings shown adjoining the house were the carpenter's shop, stables, cart house and storeroom.

Four
Alfold to Loxwood

Sidney Wood Lock House, viewed here in 1952, lay adjacent to Lock XV and was also the canal company's main workshop. John Cole and his family lived there for over thirty years in the mid-nineteenth century carrying out all manner of repairs, constructing lock-gates and building boats.

The site of Lock XV lay on the other side of the crossing point in the centre of this recent picture. The former lock house and garden are of course private property and must not be visited without permission.

High Bridge at Alfold. Rosemary Lane leads from Alfold Village to Sidney Farm and formerly crossed over the canal at High Bridge, whose site is to the right of the private dwelling (built many years after the waterway was closed). The farm was the site of Sidney Mill, which was connected with the local ironworks, as indicated by the local place names Furnace Bridge and Burningfold Wood.

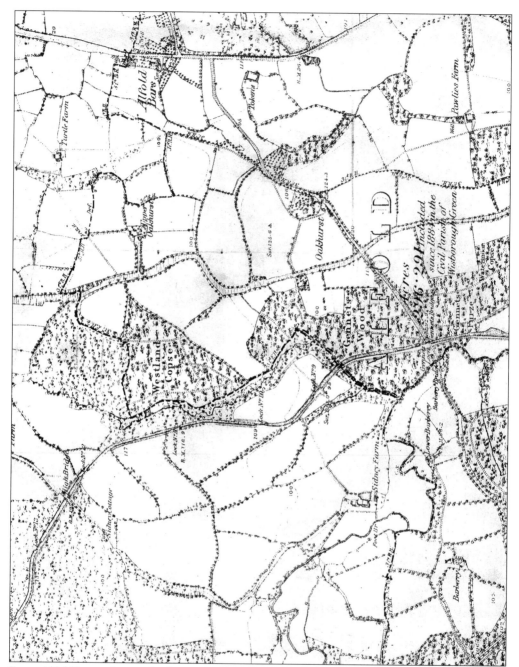

From Alfold barges began the descent to the English Channel. In the space of ten furlongs, nine locks lowered the water level by 63ft. The 1870 Ordnance Survey shows the location of the locks. In Gennet's Wood, a rural location 58 3/4 miles from London Bridge and 1 1/2 miles north of Loxwood, the canal crosses the county border from Surrey into West Sussex, where the water level is exactly 100ft above sea level.

Gennet's Wood, Loxwood, in 1964, looking north and showing the rise of the land as the canal heads for Guildford and the Thames. In 1964 the nearest one could approach to the lost canal was by walking along the edge of the field which bordered Gennet's Wood and climbed towards High Bridge.

The canal trust has begun clearance of the undergrowth between High Bridge and Gennet's Wood but no locks have yet been rebuilt. This view shows the recently restored section between Lock IX and Gennet's.

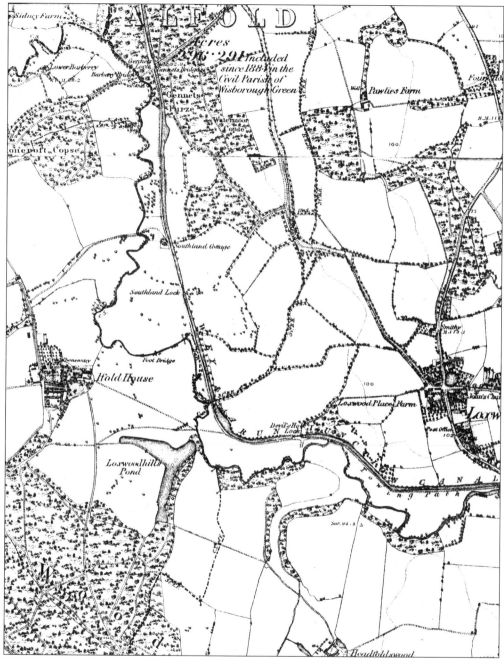

Ifold House, Loxwood, the country seat of the Napper family. It was John Napper who was chairman of the canal company from 1855 to 1867 and who in August 1859 led a deputation to meet the directors of the London, Brighton & South Coast Railway to enquire whether they wished to build a line from Guildford to Pulborough using part of the canal bed. Ifold House was demolished in 1936.

Left and below: Southlands Lock, Loxwood, is seen here being dismantled in 1927 under the supervision of Mr Walter Nash, the farm manager of the landowner Mr L. Smith and also one of the Elders of the Dependents Chapel (Cokelers) of Loxwood, a religious sect founded in 1838 by William Bridges. The old lock bricks were sold to Warners of Cranleigh and were used in the building of Turtles Farmhouse in Rosemary Lane, Alfold.

Devil's Hole Lock, Loxwood, photographed on 21 August 1891. This is the earliest known picture of the canal. In spite of much diligent research, no painting or drawing of a barge working on the Wey & Arun Junction Canal has yet been found.

The northern end of Devil's Hole Lock was partly demolished by the Royal Canadian Engineers when practising the laying of explosives before taking part in the disastrous Dieppe raid in August 1942. This view was taken in 1952.

The reconstruction of Devil's Hole Lock and Bridge in 1999.

Devil's Hole Lock, Loxwood, undergoing restoration in 1999. The size of the stone blocks explains why the lock chambers have remained in such fine condition for 180 years.

The approach to Devil's Hole Lock from Loxwood shows the extent to which this part of the waterway has been restored. The ancient excavation – of uncertain origin – known as the Devil's Hole lies to the north of the canal below the lock.

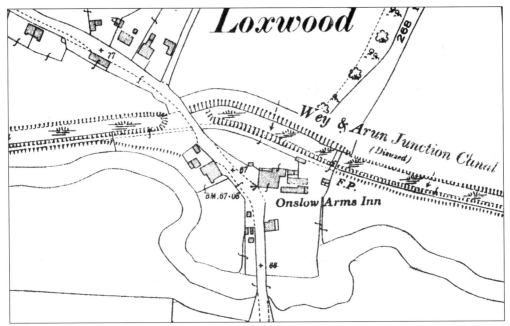

A plan of Loxwood in 1912. The canal's reedy bed is still much in evidence but the road bridge over the canal is now shown as a levelled causeway. On the north side of the canal, below the figure 77, stood a small warehouse for barge goods, a building now used by a furniture maker.

The Onslow Arms in Loxwood is at left, the former turnpike toll house at centre. The turnpike gate was removed in 1876 but the cottage was not demolished until 1962 when both the bridge over the river and the road were widened. The road bridge over the canal, demolished in 1893, would have appeared between the bank at left and north of the bungalow at right.

Five
Loxwood to Drungewick

The Onslow Arms Inn, built *c.*1800, was listed in the Oarman's Guide to the Thames and other rivers in 1857 as offering 'three beds or so' and being the only stopping place between Bramley and Pulborough. Connie Bayley relates in her book *Ifold, Loxwood & Plaistow* (1988) how during the heyday of the canal there were odd jaunts by barge from the Onslow Arms by some of the Loxwood people. It is related that the bargemaster Cox made his last voyage to Pulborough in 1874, one of the passengers being Mrs Realff of Station Road.

Celebrating the reopening of the canal from Loxwood to Drungewick Lane, the Rt Hon. Francis Maude MP is aboard the Wey & Arun Canal Trust's excursion boat at the Onslow Arms landing stage at Loxwood on 3 May 1998. Sir Michael Marshall in the bow.

Approaching Brewhurst Lock, 1999. The towpath has been resurfaced but horse riding has added considerably to its wear and tear. The trip boat *Zachariah Keppell* lies moored for the winter.

Brewhurst Lock, Loxwood, as it appeared in 1952, with both sets of lock gates precariously hanging unopened after eighty years disuse. Note the size of the trees growing out of the crevices between the blocks of Pulborough stone.

The canal trust's aim is the 'preservation, restoration and conservation' of the lost link between the rivers Wey and Arun. Since its original formation as a society in 1970 the trust has attracted 1,200 members. Here at Brewhurst Lock is one of its information notice boards which are being erected along those parts of the waterway that are a public right of way to inform the visitor of the canal's historical importance and to attract new members.

The reopening of Brewhurst Lock, Loxwood, by the Rt Hon. Francis Maude MP, Shadow Chancellor of the Exchequer, 3 May 1998.

Although the closure of the canal passed unlamented, by the turn of the century local historians were referring to it as being a picturesque reminder of a past age. Various writers wrote that what commerce had lost by its disuse had been gained by the picturesque, for nature has done her best to make man's neglected waterway her own. This 1952 view of Brewhurst Lock reflects that charm.

How the approach to Brewhurst Lock appears in 1999 now that restoration has been completed.

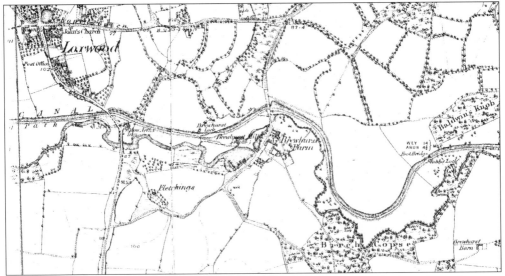

The 1870 Ordnance Survey map indicated the importance of the Onslow Arms Inn and Brewhurst Farm and Mill and identified the exact location of Brewhurst and Stubbs Locks.

The Botting family were millers at Brewhurst Mill from 1815 until 1920. Colonel E.L. Botting related how his great-uncle Tom was drowned at the age of twelve between Brewhurst Lock and the Onslow Arms on 25 January 1827. The corn mill was burnt down in the late nineteenth century and was replaced by the present mill, depicted here in 1952.

A group photograph of five vice-presidents of the Wey & Arun Canal Trust. Left to right: Sir Michael Marshall, the author, Peter Beresford, John Wood and Peter Longley, together with the present chairman and owner of Brewhurst Mill, Peter Foulger. The occasion was the reopening of the canal from Loxwood to Drungewick Lane in May 1998.

A crowded waterways scene between Brewhurst Lock and the Onslow Arms, taken at the time of the reopening of this stretch of canal in May 1998.

A recent view of the South Eastern Electricity Board's electric powered launch *Seeway* near Barnsill Bridge, reflecting the use of the new facility for pleasure boating along the waterway.

The Inland Waterways Association have given much support to the trust's efforts to restore the waterway and are seen here participating in the 1996 small boat rally.

Baldwin's Knob (or Stubbs) Lock, Loxwood. Baldwin's Knob is the name of the adjoining copse; Mr Stubbs was the farmer and landowner. Remnants of the upper gates remained in 1952 but the lower part of the chamber was a confused mass of undergrowth. Note that all the lock chambers below Southlands were built of blocks of Pulborough stone.

Baldwin's Knob Lock, Loxwood, after restoration by the canal trust. Altogether the trust had restored seven locks by 1999.

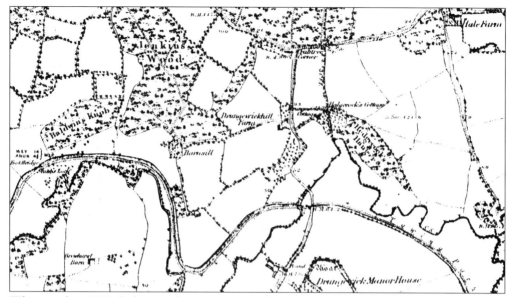

Whereas the 1870 Ordnance Survey map marks the location and names of the locks, it identifies neither Drungewick Aqueduct nor Drungewick Lane, which are located to the left of the manor house.

The trust's trip boat moored above Barnsill bridge, built by the landowner at his own expense in 1989 to gain access to farmland divided by the canal. The bridge was designed by engineering consultant Richard Lamey.

The towpath leading up to Barnsill bridge has been resurfaced by the trust and now forms an unbroken footway from High Bridge at Alfold to Drungewick Lane, a distance of 3½ miles. Note the silhouette of the author taking the photograph.

Approaching Drungewick Lane is the 1999 terminus of the canal. It is hoped to extend the present channel by bridging the Loxwood stream by an aqueduct and building a new bridge to gain access to Drungewick Lock.

The site of Drungewick Aqueduct looking towards Loxwood, showing the stone abutments of the former towpath and the dry bed of the canal at right.

PETWORTH RURAL DISTRICT COUNCIL

DRUNGEWICK BRIDGE
AND ROAD.

NOTICE IS HEREBY GIVEN THAT THIS ROAD will be CLOSED FROM THIS DATE TO ALL THROUGH TRAFFIC during the pulling down of the present Bridges over the River and the Canal and the building of a New Bridge over the River near Drungewick.

The Road will still be available for Local Traffic as far as the Bridges.

By order of the Council.

GEORGE T. SUTEM,

Surveyor,

The Mill, Petworth,
July 3rd, 1908.

Plans are now well advanced for approving the contract to build the new aqueduct over the western branch of the River Arun (River Lox) and to rebuild the road bridge (demolished in 1907) over the canal. The cost is estimated in the region of £600,000 and it is hoped to begin work in the year 2000.

Six

Drungewick to Newbridge

Although unused since 1871, Drungewick Aqueduct was still largely intact when this photograph was taken in 1932. G.D. Johnston described it as having 'three low flat arches and a solid parapet of red brick, the arches rimmed with four tiers of bricks and the parapet capped with white stone'. However, it was noted that the left arch was beginning to collapse and the north side had lost its parapet.

Roger Sellman found little change in the condition of Drungewick Aqueduct when he took this photograph in 1934 to illustrate his article in the *Sussex County Magazine*.

By August 1952 the north face of Drungewick Aqueduct had collapsed and the autumn floods that year washed away the remaining arches.

The site of Drungewick Aqueduct in 1955 looking towards Drungewick Lane. Note the closed gate on the former towpath. The Southern Water Authority has now realigned the course of the river at this point so the canal will also follow a slightly different route when reconstructed.

In October 1998 planning consent was granted to replace the former aqueduct and road bridge over the canal at Drungewick, albeit by a slightly different route. Known as the Loxwood Link Extension Project, about 60% of the total cost has already been promised and if all goes well the work should be completed by the year 2001.

PROPOSED DEVELOPMENT

NOTICE UNDER SECTIONS 65 OF THE TOWN AND COUNTRY PLANNING ACT 1990 AND THE TOWN AND COUNTRY PLANNING (GENERAL DEVELOPMENT PROCEDURE) ORDER 1995.

NOTICE OF APPLICATION FOR PLANNING PERMISSION

NOTICE IS HEREBY GIVEN that an application has been made to Chichester District Council for the following description of development:

REFERENCE:

(P) LX/98/01083/FUL

PROPOSAL:

Proposed aqueduct and roadbridge and restoration of section of canal channel.

LOCATION:

Land At Junction Of Wey & Arun Canal And Drungewick Lane Loxwood Billingshurst West Sussex

The application and plans may be inspected at the Planning and Building Control Department, East Pallant House, East Pallant Chichester between 8.45am and 5.10pm Mondays to Thursdays and between 8.45am and 5.00pm Fridays. In addition for applications north of the Downs plans are available for inspection at the Council Offices at Midhurst [applications marked (M)] and Petworth [applications marked (P)] between 9.00am and 12.30pm and 1.30pm and 4.30pm Mondays to Thursdays and between 9.00am and 12.30pm and 1.30pm and 4.00pm Fridays.

Any representations should be made to the address below by not later than 16.09.98. Please note that the Council does not acknowledge receipt of your letter but you will be notified of the decision.

A J Howes BA;DipLP;MRTPI
Director of Planning and Strategic Services
East Pallant House
East Pallant
CHICHESTER PO19 1TY

A view of the canal bed approaching Drungewick Lock in 1952. Although the towpath had been cleared, the bed has now a much reedier appearance.

The interior of Drungewick Lock as it appeared in March 1952...

...and during the winter of 1963, when the size of the trees in the lock chamber is certainly larger.

The view beneath the bridge at the tall end of Drungewick Lock looking north. When these pictures were taken in March 1952 the remains of the gates standing since the 1860s could be seen lying in the water.

In this 1952 view of Drungewick Lock the hinge post of the lock gate can be seen standing at left.

Drungewick Lock, Loxwood. The chamber has been cleared by the canal trust and the walls rebuilt awaiting the completion of the new aqueduct. When this has been completed it is expected that it will not be long before boats can reach Newbridge. However it may take a little longer to reach Pallingham and complete the route to the sea at Littlehampton.

The view of the entrance to Drungewick Lock from the south in 1955. Drungewick Manor House once belonged to the Abbey of Seez but was sold around 1700 to Sir Edward Onslow, whose descendant the second earl, Thomas Onslow, was MP for Guildford 1784-1806, one of the original shareholders in the canal company and present at the opening celebrations in 1816.

The view of the entrance to Drungewick Lock approaching from the south as it now looks in 1999.

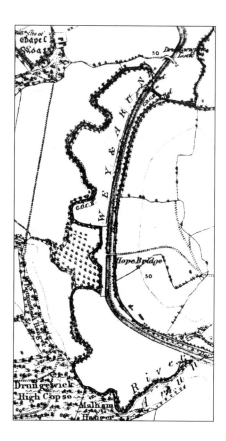

Just below Drungewick Lock the 1870 Ordnance Survey reveals the first of the two diversions which had to be made to the River Arun. The former course of the river is at left.

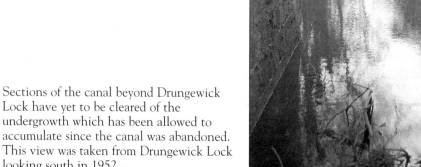

Sections of the canal beyond Drungewick Lock have yet to be cleared of the undergrowth which has been allowed to accumulate since the canal was abandoned. This view was taken from Drungewick Lock looking south in 1952...

94

…and this one in 1999.

Hope Farm Bridge at Rudgwick. When the canal was built the River Arun was diverted by a new cut, which ran parallel to the canal. This saved building two aqueducts over the river. The arch of the canal bridge built in 1815 had fallen when this picture was taken in March 1952 and was later replaced by a causeway leading to the meadows bordering the cut-off loops of the old river.

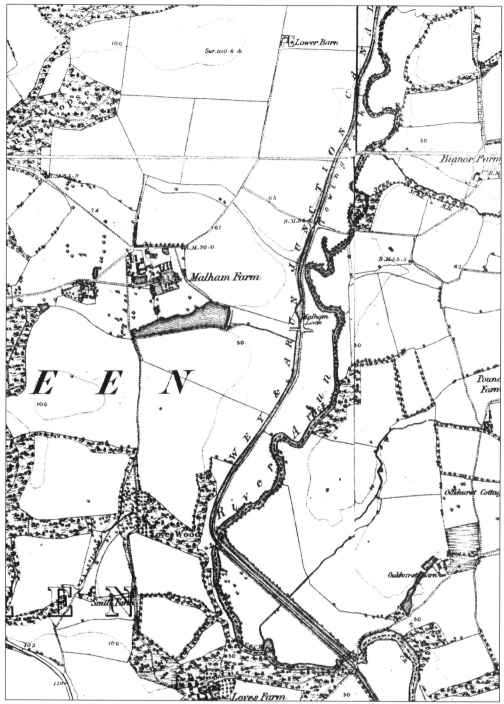

The 1870 Ordnance Survey shows the feeder stream from the lake at Malham Farm entering the canal below the lock. Further south another bend of the River Arun was cut off to avoid building two aqueducts.

Malham Lock, Wisborough Green, has been restored. The gates will not be installed until the upper reaches of the canal have been cleared and watered.

Loves Farm Bridge, Wisborough Green, was the site of another accommodation bridge over the canal to give access to the meadow land cut off from the farm by its construction. This new bridge was built by the canal trust and reopened in 1975.

Rowner Mill, Billingshurst, was a fine water mill whose weir bestrode the River Arun and which lay due east of, and parallel to, Rowner Lock. This view dates from the turn of the century. The mill was totally gutted by fire in the late 1950s.

This view of Rowner Lock was taken in 1907, thirty-six years after the last barge had passed through from London. In 1982 the lock was the first to be restored by the Wey & Arun Canal Trust and it is now in working order. The River Arun marks the boundary between the parishes of Billingshurst and Wisborough Green, which accounts for the incorrect title on the postcard.

Rowner Lock and Lock House, 1843. Charles Baverstock was the lock-keeper (1824-1871). His family kept bees and sold freshly baked bread, butter, honey and home-made ginger beer to the bargees as well as assisting in collecting the tolls on up traffic. The lock house, which contained two upper rooms and three lower rooms was later occupied by the Hosgrove family but after their departure it fell into ruin and was demolished in the 1940s.

Rowner Lock viewed before restoration in 1971. One of the peculiarities of derelict lock chambers is the way ferns and trees find a natural habitat in the crevices between the stone blocks.

Rowner Lock was restored and reopened by the Wey & Arun Canal Trust in 1982. Jim Rendall draws the paddles, Richard Lamey is in the punt and Joy Wood holds the rope as the lock is filled for the first time in over 100 years.

Northlands Lifting Bridge, Wisborough Green, did not exist in the days when the canal was in commercial use. However, around 1960 a reinforced concrete bridge was built for the passage of farm machinery across the canal. Although the bridge span was 14ft, headroom was only one foot above water level. As it was not practicable to build a new fixed bridge with an 8'6' headroom, Owen Jones designed a lifting bridge of the type much used on the Shropshire canals. The concrete bridge was removed and the new bridge completed in August 1980.

Above and below: Newbridge, Wisborough Green, was the terminal point of the Wey & Arun Junction Canal. The canal bridge constructed in 1815 carried the turnpike road from Guildford to Pulborough and Arundel as well as being the main highway between Billingshurst, Wisborough Green and Petworth. These photographs were taken in 1953 when the bridge was undergoing emergency support to carry the heavy traffic on the A272. Note the towpath on the right-hand side. The adjacent bridge over the river was built in the eighteenth century although previous 'new bridges' had been built here at varying times since the thirteenth century.

Wisborough Green lies just over one mile from Newbridge. It was an important village in the nineteenth century. Although from the 1790s carters brought coal and goods from Newbridge Wharf that had been barged up from Arundel, it was not until 1816 that the village stores began to receive regular supplies of groceries and merchandise from London. The population of the village hardly changed during the time the canal was in operation; in 1821 it was 1,679 and fifty years later it had only risen to 1,756. In 1901, shortly after the time when this picture was taken, there were still only 1,585 inhabitants.

During the period when Newbridge Wharf was, as William Cobbett described it, 'a grand receiving and distributing place', the wharfinger kept a beer house known locally as the Limeburners. The licence had been granted by the local bench in 1805 after the Arun Navigation proprietors had stated that it would be of great benefit to merchants transacting business as well as to the public. After the navigation was closed, this reverted to a private dwelling and the inn situated within a mile of the wharf on the road to Adversane adopted the name.

Billingshurst was an important village in the nineteenth century, situated on Stane Street, the Roman road from Chichester to London, and less than two miles from Newbridge Wharf. Before the canal opened the population was 1,295 (1811) but by 1831 it had risen to 1,540. The village was an important centre of the hoop industry. Hoops were sent regularly by barge up to London for use in making beer casks and down to Arundel where they were dispatched to the northern ports for fish trade. This drawing was made in 1843.

It was at the King's Arms in Billingshurst High Street that in July 1867 the intrepid pleasure boater J.B. Dashwood, accompanied by his wife and dog, lodged for the night. Its hospitality left nothing to be desired. Dashwood was full of praise for this 'neat, clean inn' where everything was to his satisfaction. For dinner there were 'mutton chops done to a turn with excellent beer and very fine sherry'. Next morning the little inn was in a bustle by five o'clock – 'hot and cold water for shaving, and baths, to any amount, and boots polished like mirrors. The breakfast was a capital one, and as punctual as we could wish; for our little table saw its cold meat, eggs, toast and coffee awaiting us at the given hour of 5.45 am.'

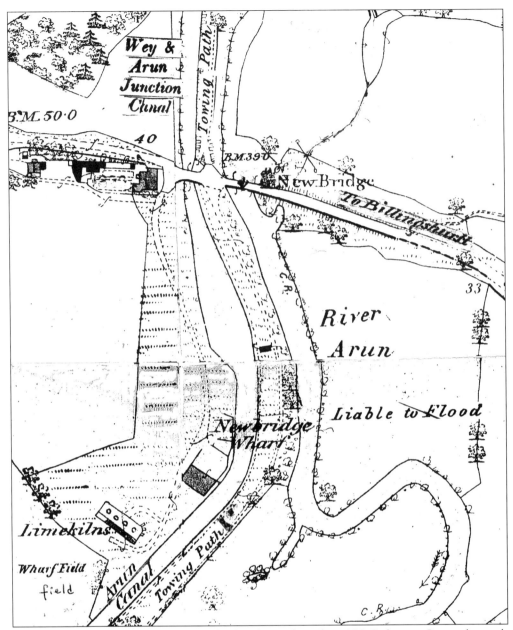

The former wharfinger's house at Newbridge, located on the 1876 Ordnance Survey beneath the figure 40, was situated at the entrance to Newbridge Wharf. In 1842 the house was owned by the Arun Navigation Company and occupied by Richard Seward who was both the canal's superintendent and wharfinger (1828-1856) and was listed as the occupier of the beer shop and garden. By 1878 Thomas Stringer had become a beer retailer but by 1887 one of the buildings was listed as a shop.

Six

Newbridge to Stopham (Arun Navigation)

The only known photograph of barges on the Arun Canal shows Fred (standing on the bank) and Walter Dunkerton below Newbridge *c.*1885. Their father, George Dunkerton, was wharfinger from 1868 to 1886, by which time there was so little traffic that the arrangement was discontinued. The canal was closed in 1888 and sometime in the 1890s the family moved to Wheelers Farm in Wisborough Green where they began a dairy business. Whereas barges on the Wey & Arun were given names, those on the Arun Navigation were known by their licence number as seen here.

Newbridge Wharf, the terminus of the Arun Navigation. In August 1823 William Cobbett passed by. 'Soon after quitting Billingshurst', he wrote, 'I crossed the River Arun, which has a canal running alongside of it. At this there are large timber and coal yards, and kilns for lime. This appears to be a grand receiving and distributing place'. Billingshurst and the surrounding farms and villages looked to the wharf at Newbridge for the arrival of their coal and groceries, for their fertilizers and fancy goods from London, Guildford and Arundel, and as the most convenient means of dispatching their own wares and farm produce to market.

The Arun Canal between Newbridge and Pallingham (4½ miles) was used by barge traffic from 1787 until 1888. It was operated independently of the Wey & Arun Canal and remained open for seventeen years longer. The warehouse was built in 1839 when barge traffic was at its busiest. After the closure of the canal, it was used as a farm store until purchased by Mr David Mitchell. It has now been converted into a luxury guest house.

The east elevation of the warehouse was photographed in January 1963 when the ice across the canal was so thick that the author was able to skate around the tree trunks growing in the canal bed.

Newbridge Wharf. After the closing of the junction canal, the Arun proprietors suffered an inevitable diminution of trade. Toll receipts had fallen by more than three quarters from £1,066 in 1864 to only £255 in 1873, representing a drop in tonnage of nearly two thirds. The company's decision to cease being wharfingers was therefore an inevitable economy.

ARUN NAVIGATION.

NEWBRIDGE WHARF.

NOTICE

IS HEREBY GIVEN, THAT

ON AND AFTER THE 1st OF APRIL, 1874,

THE

ARUN NAVIGATION PROPRIETORS

Will cease to be Wharfingers or receive or deliver Goods at NEWBRIDGE WHARF, in the Parish of Wisbro' Green, or be answerable for any Goods deposited there; the Wharf may, however, still be used at the risk of the Persons using the same.

Dated this 1st day of December, 1873,

(BY ORDER)

EDWARD ARNOLD,

CLERK TO THE PROPRIETORS.

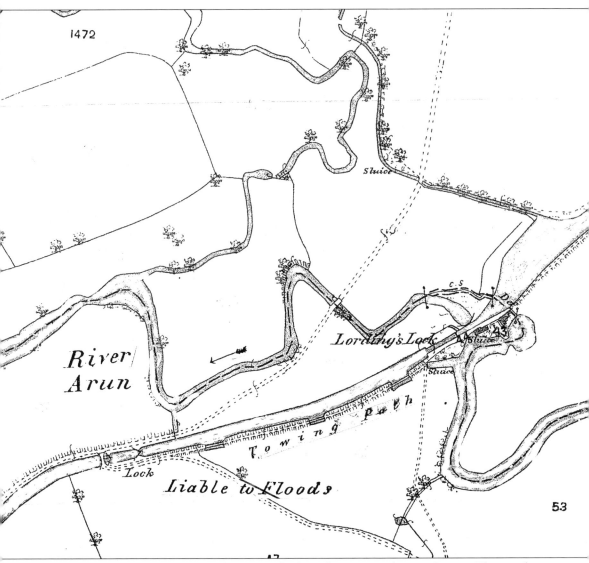

Lording's Lock and Orfold aqueduct as marked on the 1876 Ordnance Survey. The winding hole above the lock was fed by the tributary stream seen at the top right-hand corner, which flowed down from Kirdford. The lock-keeper's cottage and adjacent waterwheel, chamber and pump house are marked as numbers 43 and 44 on the map. The lock at the bottom left-hand corner was a flood lock with a one-foot rise, which had been built in 1823 to increase the draught to the aqueduct. The area was notorious for being flooded in winter when barge traffic was often halted for weeks.

The weir controlling the flow of water through the culverts under Orfold Aqueduct. The waterwheel chamber can be seen to the right of the weir paddles in this 1957 photograph.

A 1953 view of the three culverts carrying the River Arun beneath Orfold Aqueduct, seen from the opposite side to the previous picture.

The lower section of Lording's Lock beyond the aqueduct, looking toward the flood lock in 1957. It was this area that was most subject to severe flooding and breached embankments.

The site of the former accommodation bridge and lower gates of what were described in the 1821 Act of Parliament as a 'second pair of flood gates at Harford (*sic*) to form a one foot lock'. This was the only turf-sided lock on the navigation. The work of excavating the site at Orfold was carried out by Winston Harwood and his team of volunteers in 1994.

The remains of the lower gate of the flood lock in 1952. The lock was built in 1823 to help heavily laden barges to enter Orfold Lock. This was part of the improvements required to meet the expected increase in traffic upon the opening of the Portsmouth & Arundel Canal.

An 1896 picture of the brick and stone accommodation bridge built in 1787 below the turf-sided flood lock at Lording's (Orfold), Wisborough Green. (Francis Frith photograph courtesy of Worthing Central Library)

John Stepney, who lived on the banks of the Arun Canal at Hay Barn on the Lee Place Estate, was the last man to work a barge up from Pulborough to Newbridge Wharf, where its timbers were broken up and burnt in 1888. This photograph was taken in 1952 when John was eighty-six years of age.

Lee Farm (Middle) Lock had one of its lower gates and the frame of its single upper gate still standing in 1952, more than sixty years after the last barge had passed by. The lock was also known as Middle Lock because it was the second of the three between Pallingham and Newbridge. The locks on the Arun Canal were five inches narrower and three inches shorter than those on the Wey & Arun Canal. They had only a single, instead of a double, upper gate.

The brick and stone accommodation bridges over the Arun Canal above Pallingham remained standing until the 1960s. The pictures show Lee Place Bridge (1952)…

…Lee Farm (Middle) Lock Bridge (1952)…

…and Toat Farm Bridge (1952). These have now all been repaired or reconstructed by the Wey & Arun Canal Trust with the help of the local landowners.

Cookes Bridge was an accommodation bridge to the south of Toat Farm built in 1787. By 1952 it had lost its parapet although its arch and abutments had survived. The bridge was saved from collapse by a team of voluntary workers led by Richard Lamey and Keith Ellis in 1981.

The Wey & Arun Canal Trust
assisted the Pulborough Society in
1976 in restoring the humpback
bridge built in 1786 over the Arun
Canal at Pallingham Quay. The
docks situated below the bridge
remain unrestored.

This sluice at Pallingham Lock is
located immediately above the upper
gates. When the iron lock paddle
was winched up, the water drained
into the lock chamber from the
canal pound to fill the lock. Note
the brick-lined floor of the lock
chamber in this 1952 view.

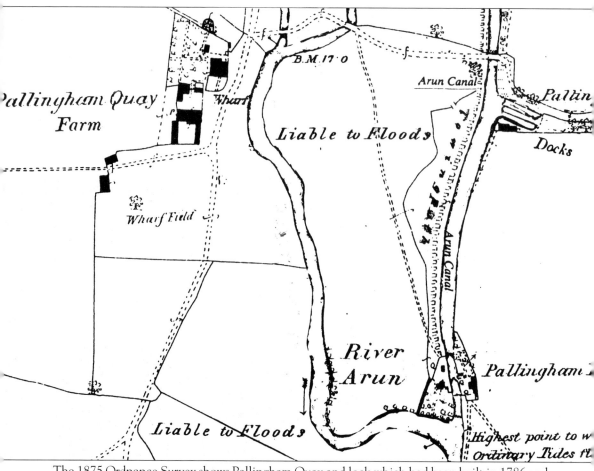

The 1875 Ordnance Survey shows Pallingham Quay and lock which had been built in 1786 and the barge building and repair yard that opened in 1804. The building marked south of the two docks was the carpenter's shop, built of timber and thatch. The quay on the River Arun had been used since the reign of Queen Elizabeth for conveying timber by barge down to Arundel, hence the name 'Wharf Field'.

The entrance to Pallingham Lock photographed in 1918. From 1792 the lock cottage was always occupied by a member of the Stone family. James Stone was lock-keeper for thirty-nine years from 1832 until 1871 when his son Benjamin took his place. The mooring posts are clearly visible as well as the pleasure boat used by Ben Stone, seen wearing his black hat.

Benjamin Stone was lock-keeper at Pallingham Lock from 1871 to 1888. He kept a carpenter's shop while his wife, Annie, ran a bakery and grocery store by the adjacent docks. They both continued to live at the lock cottage until shortly before their death. Annie died on 25 February 1933 aged eighty-four.

Ben died on 31 August 1935 and is buried with his wife in Pulborough churchyard.

Pallingham Lock House, where tolls were collected by five members of the Stone family from the time of the opening of the Arun Canal until its closure in 1888. In 1911 the house contained a living room with cupboard, a kitchen and a scullery with fireplace. Upstairs were three tiny bedrooms, one with a fireplace. On the adjacent wharf were located storerooms, a privy, a fowl-house and a small stable. This view taken in 1952 shows the lock-keeper's old skiff leaning against the wall. The extensions at each end of the house were remodelled in the late 1930s.

Pallingham Lock, built in 1789, was one of the deepest locks between Littlehampton and Weybridge, having a rise and fall of seven to nine feet depending on the amount of water coming down the river and the tide. This view dates from 1934.

The entrance to Pallingham Lock was still navigable in 1952 but the brickwork was becoming increasingly fragmented. The lock entrance is currently blocked by undergrowth and the chamber requires dredging.

Pallingham Double Lock. Heavily laden barges had insufficient water to enter the lock so before the opening of the Portsmouth & Arundel Canal it was agreed to increase the draught. A lower lock was constructed in 1822, which increased the depth of water over the cill by 18in. The remains of the lower gateposts can be seen in this 1934 photograph.

ARUN NAVIGATION.

NOTICE.

The Navigation will be

CLOSED

on and from the 1st day of January, 1888, the Traffic being insufficient to meet the working expenses.

BY ORDER,

Chichester,

13th December, 1887.

EDWARD ARNOLD,

CLERK.

Notice of Closure of the Arun Canal. After the closing of the Wey & Arun Junction Canal, traffic on the Arun Canal continued to decline. However the company made every effort to keep the navigation open. In 1882 forty-five ash and oak trees at Newbridge and Middle Lock were sold for £52. In 1883 the proprietors voluntarily contributed a similar sum to augment the dwindling receipts. The toll on coal cargoes was reduced to 3d a ton in 1885. Although no material revival of trade was expected, it was urged that keeping the canal open was in the public interest as it tended to keep down the railway rates. Revenue continued to decline so the proprietors ordered the notice of closure to be posted along the towpath in December 1887.

Railway and Canal Traffic Act, 1888.

River Arun Navigation.

APPLICATION FOR ABANDONMENT OF THE NAVIGATION.

Whereas The Company of Proprietors of the River Arun Navigation have applied to the Board of Trade, pursuant to section 45, sub-section 1, of the above Act, that the said Board of Trade should by Warrant signed by their Secretary authorise the abandonment of the Navigation belonging to the said Company, known as the River Arun Navigation, and the Canal forming part of such Navigation, by the existing Proprietors of the same, on the ground that the said Navigation and Canal are unnecessary for the purposes of Public Navigation within the meaning of the said section, and should make an order releasing the said Company or other the Proprietors of the Navigation and Canal from all liability to maintain the Navigation and Canal and from all statutory and other obligations in respect thereof or of or consequent on the abandonment thereof.

And Whereas the Board of Trade have directed Inquiry to be held by an Assistant Secretary of the Board of Trade into the subject matter of the said application for abandonment and to determine the amount of compensation (if any) to be paid to all persons entitled to compensation by reason of the proposed abandonment.

Notice is hereby given, that FRANCIS JOHN STEPHENS HOPWOOD, Esquire, C.M.G., the Assistant Secretary of the Board of Trade appointed to hold the said Inquiry, will attend for that purpose at the Norfolk Arms Hotel, Arundel, on Wednesday, the Fifteenth day of November, one thousand eight hundred and ninety-three, at eleven o'clock in the forenoon, and will then and there be prepared to hear and to receive the evidence of any person interested in the matter of the said Inquiry.

Dated this   day of
one thousand eight hundred and ninety-three.

EDWARD ARNOLD,
Chichester.   CLERK.

Notice of Application for Abandonment, 1893. Although the Arun Canal had ceased to operate, it could not be abandoned until the Board of Trade had issued a warrant. Before it could do this a public enquiry had to be held, and when held in Arundel there were nine objections to the winding-up order. Not until September 1896 was the warrant obtained.

Sam Strudwick (1864-1933) standing (at right) in his newly built barge *Reliance of Fittleworth* above Stopham Bridge in 1905. This barge, 72ft by 12ft, replaced the *Eleanor*, which he had inherited from his father, bargemaster John Strudwick (1821-1903), who could remember working on the Portsmouth & Arundel Canal in the 1830s.

Sam Strudwick's partner, Loyal Saigeman, on the *Reliance* above Stopham Bridge, 1905. His average load was thirty-three tons. The principal consignments were chalk, coal, culm, gravel and sand, but from time to time the *Reliance* carried bricks down to Littlehampton, steam coal up to Arundel, bolts of reeds and osiers for Pepper & Son at Houghton, gas coal to Greatham and flints for the Duke of Norfolk at Timberley and for the Rector of Pulborough.

Stopham Bridge. Built during the reign of King Edward II (1307-1327) a drawbridge facilitated the passage of boats in the seventeenth century. In 1822 the central arch was raised to allow more heavily laden barges to pass in connection with the London to Portsmouth trade. The boathouse was built soon after the turn of the century, and much used at the time of the local regatta. Only its foundations remained after the great flood in 1968. This oil painting by Henry King dates from before the First World War.

No.64 below Pulborough Bridge in August 1900 with Bargemaster Henry Doick (1847-1902) and his sons Percy and Tom. In the space of seven years (1895-1901) he made 521 voyages up and down the Arun carrying 17,096 tons of cargo between Littlehampton and Pulborough. For thirty years he was one of the bell-ringers at Pulborough church.

Bargemaster Sam Strudwick was one of the last carriers on the Arun Navigation. This view of the *Reliance* was taken in 1913. She was sold to the Arun Brick Company in 1923 and in 1925 the harbourmaster at Littlehampton reported that it had been agreed that the abandoned barge should be given to the Commissioners in return for its removal from the tideway.

Acknowledgements

I should like to thank John Wood and other members of the Wey & Arun Canal Trust for their assistance in completing this work.

The staff of both the Surrey and the West Sussex County Record Offices, as well as Matthew Alexander of Guildford Museum, Janet Austin of Loxwood, and Martin Hayes of the West Sussex County Library Service, have complemented this effort.

Kay Bowen has been responsible for ensuring that the author walked the whole line of navigation and for the typing of the captions. Edwina Vine also helped in many ways.

The WEY·SOUTH **PROJECT**

The Wey & Arun Canal Trust

The Trust warmly welcomes new members.
There are opportunities for hands-on restoration with the working parties as well as crewing the trip boat, helping at a sales stall or publicity etc.
All members receive the quarterly bulletin *Wey-South*.

For membership details and latest information, apply to:
The Office Manager,
The Wey & Arun Canal Trust,
The Granary, Flitchfold Farm, Vicarage Hill,
Loxwood, BILLINGSHURST, West Sussex RH14 0RH.
Tel/Fax: 01403 752403
E-mail: wact@weyandarun.freeserve.co.uk
Web site: http://www.wact/nu/

Enjoy a cruise on a restored section of canal at Loxwood.
Operates Saturday and Sunday afternoons from rear of the *Onslow Arms* public house, from Easter to October (subject to water supply).
Full details from above address.

Please note that the former towpath of the canal is no longer a public right of way and walkers should consult the canal trust's booklet, *The Wey-South Path*, to ascertain which sections can be followed.

Bibliography

Hadfield, Charles, *The Canals of South andSouth-East England.* (1969).
Vine, P.A.L., *London's Lost Route to the Sea.* (1996, 5th edition).

Other works by P.A.L. Vine

London's Lost Route to the Sea (1965)
London's Lost Route to Basingstoke (1968)
The Royal Military Canal (1972)
Magdala (1973)
Ethiopia (1974)
Introduction to Our Canal Population: George Smith (1974)
Pleasure Boating in the Victorian Era (1983)
British Pleasure Boating on the Continent (1984)
West Sussex Waterways (1985)
Surrey Waterways (1987)
Kent & East Sussex Waterways (1989)
Hampshire Waterways (1990)
London to Portsmouth Waterway (1994)
London's Lost Route to Basingstoke, new edition (1994)
London's Lost Route to Midhurst (1995)